A Pocketful of Crotchets

A Pocketful of Crotchets

by C M Dias

This is a work of fiction. Names, characters, places, and incidents either are the product of the author's imagination or are used fictitiously. Any resemblance to actual persons, living or dead, events, or locales is entirely coincidental.

For more information, contact: cdroses365@gmail.com

First paperback edition 2023

Published by Legato Lilt Publishing

Book design by C.M. Dias and G. Chron
Illustrated by G. Chron

978-1-80541-249-6 (paperback)
978-1-80541-251-9 (hardcover)
978-1-80541-251-9 (ebook)

A Pocketful of Crotchets

For

My Children

Natalie, Edward, Thomas, Catharine, Charles

And theirs

Theo, Marley, Rex, Sebastian, Valentina, Remy, Emilia

And for those who love to learn music

Those yet to learn to love music

And to my parents and grandparents

Whose love of music inspired mine

In appreciation of the support and guidance from

Jenny, Kostadinka, Nick, Nina, Marianne, Sally

George, whose illustrations, artistic interpretation,
skill and patience bring the story to life

Contents

1. Pitching Up

'Tap, tap, tap,' sounded the baton.

Beth's heartbeat pounded through the sudden silence. She stared blankly at the piano keys and music sheet facing her. Close by, the conductor plucked the tips of a tuning fork and held them to his ear. As he rested the end on the piano top Beth heard its note resonate. When he nodded to her, she pressed the A key, shakily at first, then harder, several times until a second nod made her stop. The violinist bowed a string, then a cacophony of sound immediately followed from instruments small and large. How did she seem to know what to do? After all, she had never played with an orchestra before. For a brief moment, she closed her eyes and thought hard.

Daring to blink them open she startled herself, for she was now standing at the professor's front door with her trusty bike and wicker basket beside her and an index finger firmly fixed on the doorbell at number ninety-seven. But the bell echoed with a familiarity that puzzled Beth. She checked her watch. 'Four-thirty!' she read, lifting her hand away. She recalled her mum telling her that the professor, as well as his many years of teaching experience, seemed 'jolly', and a 'colourful character'. Beth smiled. In front of her an untidy trail of ivy twisted and crept curiously around the wooden doorframe. She noticed that the letterbox was unusually small and wondered how anything, other than perhaps a note from a friend could ever fit through without a struggle. Beth picked at some little curls of dark green paint from the door.

However she regarded herself, eleven-year-old Beth had received a promising report from Miss Ingle, her school music teacher. Having recently passed her Grade 4 Piano as well, had led to a recommendation to Miss Ingle's friend, Professor Rubato. Beth's mum welcomed the news. She had blamed the apparent shortage of school music teachers and dwindling student numbers for hampering Beth's progress. However, there was more to it than this. Beth had not told her mum about the teasing she had to put up with during her first term at secondary school. She had been ridiculed for her enthusiasm for piano playing, with some mocking her for thinking she was *so* good. Sadly, Beth had begun to lose confidence and motivation. However, she liked Miss Ingle and had often enjoyed hearing her play the school piano, wishing that someday she would be able to play as well as her. But more importantly for Beth, she wanted to play as well as the popular girls in her school could play *their* instruments.

'Perhaps one day I could surprise them all, *and me!*' she thought. 'And since my mum's now paying for private music lessons with a *professor*, perhaps I ought, at least, to try a bit harder. What was it?…What did she write? – 'shows great promise and'… um – 'needs stretching to new musical heights,'…'er...*Really!*' she chortled, rolling her eyes. Kicking out the prop from her bicycle, she removed her helmet and swept her fringe across her warm forehead. A sudden movement at the kitchen window caught her eye, as a man snapped closed his newspaper.

'Was that him?' she wondered.

He seemed to look at something pinned to his jacket pocket and jumped to his feet. Beth stepped back quickly but kept watching the tall figure. He had a shock of untidy white hair and was dressed in a bright-blue waistcoat and jacket but moved too quickly for her to see any more. Before long he had disappeared from view. 'Woah?' she gasped, feeling a flash of nerves run from heart to stomach. She grabbed her worn leather case from the basket strapped to the handlebars and stood to attention. Just then the man opened the door with a flourish.

'Come in my *dear* girl!' he boomed, in a way quite unlike what she was expecting, and plunged into a deep theatrical bow. 'Professor Rubato's the name,' he announced cheerfully, straightening again, 'and you must be *Bethany*.... is that right?'

Beth leant in to pick up whatever it was that had fallen from the professor's jacket pocket. It was a tuning fork and the first time she had held one.

'Yes... um, Professor. I'm Beth,' she giggled quietly, as she handed it to him.

'Hello indeed!' he replied. 'And thank you... *Beth*,' he'd noted, spinning around to lead the way.

Stepping inside just as the grandfather clock chimed at half past four, Beth felt some relief that the first formalities were over. She closed the front door and swiftly caught up with him at the doorway to the sunny music room. But his welcoming gesture was largely ignored. Beth couldn't move. Ahead stood a grand piano with its lid propped fully open, commanding the far wall space and partially obscuring the garden view. Beth's jaw dropped. Her eyes followed the contours of the top edge that almost seemed to skim the chandelier above it. Its massive wooden body gracefully cradled a series of tightened strings

97

and felted hammers, inviting a closer look. But Beth hesitated.

'Er hum,' coughed the professor from a creaking chair beside the piano, 'are you joining us, Beth?'

'Oh, it's just that I only have an upright at home, … and I've never seen a grand piano close up before,' stated Beth apologetically.

'Do come and take your seat,' he smiled, patting the upholstered stool enthusiastically, and spilling puffs of vintage dust into the air.

Beth side-stepped into the room and shuffled her way along the stool, smoothing her hands over her knees in nervous excitement. The early evening light streamed through large French doors and bounced off the polished ebony piano. In front, lay silent, orderly keys. Beth leaned back slightly. Below shone three brassy pedals.

'Just like a car,' she smiled.

'I see you agree she's a *fine* instrument,' he beamed, '*and* more than one hundred years old!'

'But it's so b – *big!*' she replied, with a gaze fixed to the wooden expanse angled above.

'Oh that's *perfectly* safe – look!' he said, tugging at the supporting pole for the lid. 'Now you show me what music you've brought,' he continued, 'and I'll just get things ready.' And with that, Beth shuffled her music sheets into some order, propped them on the stand and glanced at the professor.

'Now, let me see….' he said, pulling a bright handkerchief from seemingly nowhere. Beth could now see the ancient timepiece pinned to his breast pocket as he stood rhythmically flicking away 'dust' from the keys. 'There. That should do it! Ready, Beth?' he said, admiring his work.

Beth gave half a smile as she smoothed down the centre pages of Duvernoy's Allegretto from her graded studies. Her fingers began attacking the notes with an immediacy that surprised even her.

'Got to get it right!' she repeated nervously. But, a lack of practice and some tricky fingering seemed to bewilder her, and Beth let out an audible sigh.

'Alright, let's slow it all down,' said the professor gently. 'It's Okay. You're here to learn, Beth. Try again. Really listen to the sound as you play. Okay?'

Beth leaned into the page and scrutinised the music in front of her. She fingered the notes quickly in the air before striking the keys assertively. As she did so, their rounded sounds spread further and further, filling the vacant air around her. She did it again.

'I *really* like this piano. It's like it's breathing out the music!'

'Well, I'm sure you're right, Beth,' smiled the professor.

Beth straightened and examined the blackened dots nestled comfortably between the lines. With a slow determination she continued, making fewer mistakes.

'Splendid! I knew you could do it! Carry on to the end and just remember your timing in this bar here ...' he said, reaching for a pencil and circling the fingering carefully, 'and here, too.'

'This is going well,' thought Beth, welcoming the professor's enthusiasm. 'What's next?' she wondered, instantly regretting that thought.

'Right, let's hear some scales, Beth, if you will?'

Beth quietly groaned, folding her arms and wondering if she could remember even one scale well enough. She noticed that the professor had sketched a pair of spectacles over the tricky part of the allegretto and laughed. Quickly positioning both hands on the keyboard, she was ready to play an E major.

'Right hand only, to start with please!' Beth leant forward and began playing. Her fingers performed mini somersaults – some striking the wrong keys. 'Again, please. Shoulders down. Relax, if you will.'

'Relax? Beth thought, 'but there's so much to remember!' She began attacking the notes, daring her fingers to misfire. It didn't work. She tried again.

'Now, don't get all crotchety with those crotchets,' he laughed. 'Thumb under, onto the A. Keep going while I make a quick cuppa. One for you, too?'

'Oh, no thank you,' replied Beth, a little surprised but now more determined. 'E, F sharp, G sharp, … thumb under … did it!'

Her next attempt didn't work and Beth slumped in defeat. She turned to find that the professor had left. The room was silent but for a 'tick-tock' from behind the closed door. She was now alone.

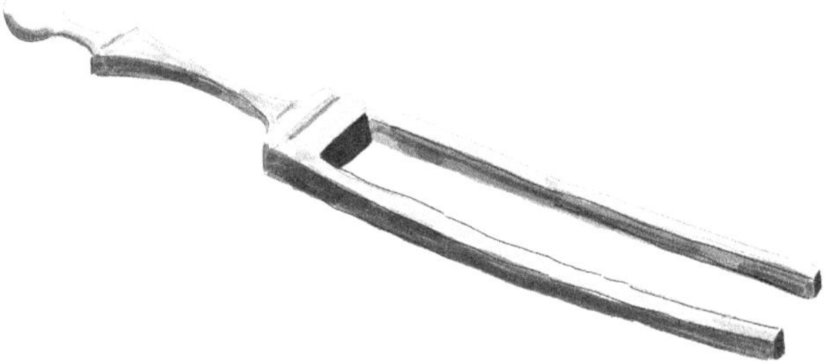

2. The Golden Manuscript

Beth looked around her. The walls were cluttered with all manner of things, piled and propped against each other. Heavy drapes hung partly across the front sash windows where an armchair, dressed in a faded throw, commanded its position. Next to it, ailing yucca plants competed for sunlight. Hanging crookedly on another wall was a patchwork of small paintings depicting country views and all looking very similar to each other. Close, but not close enough to read any detail, hung a cluster of framed certificates. She could just make out the words 'The Royal College of Music,' 'Professor Robin Rubato' and a fancy signature at the bottom.

'So, he's *Robin!*' she chuckled, raising an eyebrow as if party to some secret information. Beth noticed another certificate and stood to see it more clearly. 'The Faculty of Music,' and 'The University of Cambridge,' she read, turning cautiously to the door.

Beth moved into the large clearing in the middle of the room, stretched her arms outwards and circled slowly. As she neared the shelving, she smelled something musty, possibly from a stack of yellowing manuscripts, immersing her into the professor's past. But, nestled on the top shelf among more manuscripts, something glistened. It seemed to come from a book – the only one facing the wrong way.

'What's *that?*' she whispered, blinking hard with intrigue. Its golden edge sparkled temptingly. Her eyes darted towards the door. Lifting onto tiptoes, Beth stretched high enough to just touch it before wobbling off balance. She tried again, holding her breath as she reached. 'Got it!' she panted, 'but it's warm!' she said, as it glowed in her hands. Beth wiped her palm along her jeans before smoothing a trembling finger over the cover. She held her breath. In that instant the clock chimed. Beth gasped. 'What *is* this?' she said, gingerly lifting the cover.

'I see you've found it!' boomed the voice of the professor.

'Wah?' gasped Beth, swinging round to find him standing in the doorway, cradling a cup of tea.

'I'm sorry, Professor,' she trembled, 'I was just … just …' said Beth, tripping over her words and trying to work out how she hadn't seen him there seconds earlier.

'Blessed biscuit!' he cursed, skilfully angling a teaspoon into his mug and lifting out a soggy lump. 'No need to apologise,' he said, devouring his spoonful of sludge.

MYHAMA & STRINGS

'In fact, I couldn't be more delighted!' he chuckled.

Beth pushed her arms towards the professor as if to return the manuscript.

'Here. Sorry. But how is it doing … an . . .and what *is* it?' she stumbled, still holding tight and wondering why she wasn't in any trouble. 'I couldn't help...I saw it was glowing,' she said, her cheeks flushing.

The professor was smiling.

'Go ahead. Take a good look,' he said, washing down his biscuit before setting down his mug.

Beth passed it to him nervously. He cradled it briefly in his arms and tears welled in his dark eyes. She pulled a puzzled face as she watched. Then, lifting it gently, he blew across the hard front cover. In that single puff he had exposed a perfectly formed treble clef, embossed in gold leaf and shining exquisitely.

'Wow! It's beautiful!' Beth said, clearing her throat. 'How does it shine like that?'

The professor passed it back to her.

'Open it! Open it!' he urged, choking with joyful emotion.

Beth lifted the thick cover carefully, trying to peep beneath at first. She turned to the first, second, then third page and onto the next, until she came to an unfinished piece of handwritten music etched in black

ink. She looked up. The professor was standing next to her beaming, as if in anticipation. Beth quickly turned to the next page. As she did so, mysterious skid type marks began to appear down the page. She checked her fingers then stared at the page.

Musical notes began to cascade randomly from it, tumbling to the floor.

'What's going on?' she asked, thrusting the book into the professor's arms and stepping back. The last note joined the others, leaving an empty page. She peered down in disbelief at the notes, which seemed to have turned solid. The professor closed the book hastily and stooped low to gather them. He was chuckling loudly. Beth watched for a moment before joining him. 'Let *me!*' she laughed nervously, and crouched beside him, flicking a note about like a cat with its prey. Lifting one onto her hand she examined it, squeezing it slightly, even smelling it. 'What on earth . . .?' she croaked. It looked like a crotchet note, with a sponge-like head and thin tail. It didn't smell and it didn't move. 'Are they all the same?' she asked, finding her voice. Beth held out a handful of them to the professor. 'How did that happen? I mean they just fell off the page! I didn't mean to …' she began. Beth squeezed a note between her fingers before tipping the rest into his waiting hand.

'*You* take them, Beth. They're yours.'

'Mine? But …' Beth sensed this was something significant but was lost for words.

He gestured to her. 'Put out your hand.'

Beth cupped her hands, accepting them like a gift with no obvious use.

'But what are they? And what do I …?' she began, pushing them slowly into the side pockets of her jeans, where they formed small bulges.

'Shhh… wait and see.' smiled the professor, replacing the manuscript carefully on its shelf.

'Thank you,' is all she could find to say in that moment, but noticed he looked relieved somehow. 'But, why?' she thought, 'the glowing manuscript, golden clef, and the musical notes – if that's what they are. What does it all mean?'

As she returned to the stool, she made sure she pushed them deeper into her pockets before sitting down. During the remaining minutes of the lesson, Beth found it hard to concentrate, making her attempts at playing some arpeggios more difficult than usual. He didn't seem to mind however and began listing some practice points in her notebook for the following week. The professor stood tall. 'Now,' he beamed excitedly, 'practise hard and you will have a *very* good week.'

'Oh, I will? Yes, of course,' replied Beth making her way out. With her music case tucked underarm, instructions detailed in her notebook and a pocketful of crotchets, Beth called a swift 'goodbye' and pedalled home as fast as she could. 'Wait 'til I tell Mum,' she thought, eager to share the strange events of her lesson. 'Is she ever going to believe me though? And Ted?' she laughed. 'There's *no way* I'm going to tell an annoying little brother *like him,*' she huffed.

Beth was soon home and negotiated her way past Ted's bike left strewn across the front of the shed. 'He's *always* doing that!' she said, bursting into the kitchen, intent on complaining to her mum. In the moment, she completely forgot. 'Mum! The professor gave me some notes,' she announced, 'and *they* … I mean, and *he* said I could keep them, but they…'

'That's very nice, Bethany honey, but can I read them later? I'm just doing your tea,' replied her mum, slamming the oven door shut. 'It's about ready. Wash your hands and come and set the table please.'

Beth slumped over the sink. 'What's the point?' she thought. During teatime she was bursting to tell her mum and Ted about it but thought twice. 'What if Ted tries to feed them to the goldfish?' she wondered, discreetly checking her pockets before coming to a decision. 'I'm saying *nothing.*'

Beth hurried her tea, cleared her dishes and retreated uncharacteristically early to her bedroom, taking her music case with her. Ted and his mum looked at each other.

'What's with *her?*' said Ted.

Beth's mum called up the stairs, 'You alright, honey?'

'Yes mum!' came her quick reply. She closed her bedroom curtains, threw her music case onto her bed and slowly picked out the collection of notes from her pockets, holding each one by their tails and laying them in a row. 'Seven!' she whispered, scooping them up again. One at a time she squeezed their heads and let go, their spongy shape reforming in front of her eyes. 'Perhaps it was a test?' she thought, 'but what for?' Suddenly Beth had an idea. Emptying her music case, she tossed the contents onto the duvet beside the musical crotchets. 'Maybe the clue's in *there,*' she hoped, and searched excitedly through her notebook. 'Nothing!' she said dispiritedly, slamming it shut. 'But all I know is that Ted *mustn't* see them.' Beth scooped them all up, piled them onto a blank manuscript sheet on her bedside table and stared at them.

'*Please* Mum! Just *five more* minutes,' pleaded Ted.

'Absolutely not, you rascal!' his mum replied, chasing him up the stairs.

Alerted by Ted's muffled protests, Beth threw her school jumper over the notes *just* as her bedroom door flew wide open. Ted was standing in the doorway, giggling excitedly. His mum was standing behind him, catching her breath. Ted stepped in.

3. Practice

'Off you go!' said his mum, grabbing his arm.

'Yes, go *away* Ted,' called Beth quickly.

'Right, *sir!* … Farewell my friend!' teased Ted, saluting his sister.

His mum laughed. Beth didn't.

'Everything okay?' she asked. 'I mean, with school … and your music lesson? Was it okay? … Oh yes!' she gushed, 'you said you have some notes you wanted me to read, … from the professor?' Beth's mum headed towards an empty hanger.

'*I'll* hang it up, Mum!' burst Beth, slamming her hand over the jumper.

'Okay love, if you're sure?'

'Yes, I'm just tired, Mum, that's all.'

Beth couldn't wait to get back to her secret pile of curious little notes. She yawned loudly.

'Ok,' said her mum, unconvinced. 'We can leave it 'til tomorrow. Get a good night's sleep,' she said, planting a kiss.

'G'night Mum,' smiled Beth as the door closed. 'Phew! *That* was close!' She heard Ted's bedroom door close. 'Five … seven,' she counted, lifting the jumper cautiously. Beth thought hard. 'What are they for? What do I *do* with them?' she said, tugging at her hair and leaving knots still in knots.

Not long after, as she dived under her duvet into the darkness, her thoughts drifted to the golden glow of the manuscript, the treble clef and the cheerful professor.

'I want to practise *now!*' she thought, suddenly sitting up. 'Hmm, it's probably too late. Anyway, Ted's asleep.'

Beth resigned herself to getting to sleep so that she could solve her musical mystery first thing in the morning.

It was early when Beth awoke. She reached across to the bedside table and ran her hand gently over the page of manuscript. 'What *now?*' she sighed, swinging her legs out of bed. She began searching for the notes, willing them to appear. For a moment she froze. 'That's it! You're in for it!...Ted?' she bellowed. 'Stay out of my room!' she yelled, as she tussled with her inside-out dressing gown. Beth bolted straight towards Ted's bedroom.

'What's *the matter*, Bethany?' called her mum, disturbed by the early commotion.

'Tell him not to come into my room!'

'Shhh... Quieten down! Ted's asleep,' said her mum, narrowly missing his slippers on the landing. 'What's happened?'

'The...I mean, *he's*....' began Beth, still in a rage.

'He's what, Bethany?'

'He's taken my... no... I mean the... the um...'

'You must have been dreaming, love. It's okay. Dreams can often...'

'Doesn't matter, Mum,' Beth blurted, trying to calm herself. 'After all,' she thought, 'there's no point in trying to explain it, when I can't understand it myself'.

'Sometimes dreams can seem so real!...Ted hasn't done anything. He's still in bed!' laughed Beth's mum. 'I'll make us some breakfast.'

Beth returned to her room. 'I don't get it!' she said, picking up the page and looking at it. All of a sudden Beth realised there was printed music on the page, music that she didn't recognise, music that was definitely not there before. She scrutinised every mark. There were all kinds of notes, funny words, bar lines, a time signature, flats and rests. 'It's proper music *now!*' she laughed. 'But the professor didn't give me this? Are these the notes? Did they change into this?' Beth flicked over the page. 'Can't have.' She fled down the stairs and threw herself onto the piano stool. At the top of the page were the words, 'Allegretto grazioso.' 'Alleg … ret … to … graz,' she began. 'Wonder what *that* means for a start!' Beth suddenly remembered a book about musical terms that her Aunt Alice had given her.

'I know *exactly* where that is!' she said, running back up the stairs to the box under her bed labelled 'Useless Things.' 'Maybe not so useless,' she smiled, thumbing through. 'Here it is! It means … 'lively and gracefully!' So … now what?' She ran back down the stairs, clutching her little book, confident she could learn to be a *real* musician now. 'So, I've solved the first clue *and* I can speak Italian!' she laughed.

Beth began playing the notes G, F sharp, G … Her mum popped her head around the door. 'That's great, love!' she encouraged, 'a new piece?'

Beth nodded. Her attention was fixed to the page.

'Oh yes. Yes, it is!' came her late reply. 'Actually, the professor… well, he gave me some notes and they...'

But her mum had already left the room to prepare packed lunches. 'That's right. Sorry love,' she called. 'Is *after* school, okay? I'm already late.'

Beth's mum had two part-time jobs.

'Always busy,' sighed Beth quietly.

'Don't forget your lunch on the side here. Keep going with your practice, love. Ted? The bus will be here in five minutes. Hurry up! Your sister's waiting to take you. Bye!'

Beth watched her mum reversing down the driveway and throwing a frantic wave from her hatch-back. Beth waved back.

'Bye, Mum!' called Ted from the stairs, all too late, and casting an invisible cloak over his shoulder. He joined her.

'Ready, Batman?' teased Beth.

'Ready!'

'Okay. Hang on, Ted, I just want to play this bit...'

Beth had grasped the melody just well enough to make it stick in her mind, and that day at school, could think of little else. She doodled musical notes in her chemistry book, treble clefs in art and generally felt more purposeful.

Every day she sat at the piano learning a bit more of the unfinished piece, never forgetting to practise the graded piece and her E major. By the end of the first week, she felt she knew the easier bits well enough to play, first to her mum and then to the professor.

'Mum? Do you like my playing?'

'I was thinking that I didn't recognise that one. Did the professor start you on that?'

'Yes, he sort of did!' laughed Beth. 'Do you like it?'

''Course I do, honey. You're practising much more now. Well done.'

'Can't wait for my next lesson!'

'You're beaming, Beth! You *must* be enjoying them.'

The next week, as she stood at the doorstep of the professor's house, Beth secretly wished for a little more musical magic.

'If I just play what I've learnt and see if he realises...' she determined.

'Come in! Come in!' called the professor before Beth had even pressed the doorbell.

'Oh! Hello Professor!' came her startled reply. 'But I hadn't even pressed the ...' she began.

The professor was humming loudly. She began to pull the music sheets from her case. 'I didn't expect you to answer it so ... ' Beth immediately recognised the tune he was humming. 'That's the same one!' she spilled excitedly. 'That's it!' she shrieked, sending her papers flying. 'I've learnt it! – With *your* notes! But how did you know they wou ... ?'

'You have? You have, Beth?' he repeated, helping her gather up her music. 'Well, let's hear it!' They made their way quickly to the piano. Beth fidgeted in her seat.

'Let's begin,' he said.

'I really hope I can do this!' thought Beth. She began quickly, but very soon her playing became muddled. She stopped. The professor remained quiet and still. Beth drew in a deep breath, paused, then tried again. To her surprise, she played it with confidence and an ease that clearly pleased both of them.

'You've done it! You've done it!' he laughed. 'You *have* worked hard, Beth. Very, *very* well done!'

'But it was *your* notes that made the music,' she laughed. 'How did they *do* it?'

'Well, I guess … yes, I guess they just *can*! Now, quickly, let me hear the rest … your Allegretto and your scales, if you will, *please*.'

Beth returned immediately to her playing, encouraged by his enthusiasm.

'Splendid! Splendid! Now do it again … two octaves … no *threeee!*'

To her delight she could and did. 'Wow,' she thought. 'Practice really does help.'

'The best is still to come.'

'You mean I didn't do it right?'

'I mean, you've done us both proud, Beth. And … *we're on our way!*' he burst, leaping from his seat.

'But, but all I did was…' she began, startled by his actions.

The professor had begun waving his arms, dancing and clapping in glee. She couldn't help giggling. 'It will happen. It *will*,' he sang, 'but you need to do more. Much, much more, Beth.'

'More what, Professor? *What* do I need to do?' she implored.

'You need more of my wonderful notes to create *the best adventure* – you'll see,' he said, waltzing his way towards the manuscript book. 'Now, come and take as many as you wish,' he said throatily, offering her the open book. 'Do as you did before, Beth. Do your best and make musical mischief,' he said, turning to the manuscript.

'Really? Can I, Professor?'

'Come along. Take these.'

'I'll try just as hard,' she said happily, sweeping into her hands as many notes as would fill her small pockets. Beth hurriedly played some arpeggios until the chimes of the grandfather clock signalled the end of the lesson. She thanked the professor and left promptly. 'That was *extra extraordinary*!' beamed Beth as she pedalled her way home.

Her mum was reading the evening newspaper when Beth arrived. Ted was at a friend's house. Beth skipped into the living room.

'Good lesson, Beth?' she asked, peering briefly over her paper.

'Even better than last week!' she replied, grinning. She gave her mum the notebook to read, detailing the practice points for the next lesson and disappeared upstairs. As the evening drew in, Beth closed her bedroom door quietly and emptied her pockets onto the next sheet of manuscript paper. There were so many more notes now. She spread them out. Her mind was busy imagining what the professor could have meant by promising 'the best adventure'. She recalled him dancing happily and clapping. 'I *must* practise more,' she said, quickly turning off the bedside light.

'Now get to work,' she whispered, smiling into the night.

4. Suffolk Summer, September Surprise

'But Mum! Do I *have* to?' moaned Ted from his warm bed.

'You stayed out playing too long with Tommy. Come on! Make an effort, Ted. Last day before the holidays... and you too, young lady!' called her mum.

Beth's eyes sprang open. 'What's all this lazing about in bed?' she boomed. In she burst. 'It's a *glorious* morning! The sun is shining. The birds are singing!' Beth sat up.

'And what happened to you last night? You don't usually go to bed so early,' she said, nudging Beth on the arm. 'This is becoming a bit of a habit, love, isn't it?'

Beth surprised herself with her quick response. 'Oh, I thought that if I got to bed on time, I'd be up early to practise.'

'Practise? You've got a test today? On the last day of term? Why are you leaving it so late?' said her mum, jumping to conclusions.

'No, Mum. I mean, on the piano!'

'Oh, sorry, love. Why didn't you say? Well, that's good, isn't it? You must be getting on well with the professor. Play on!' she replied awkwardly, picking up the manuscript. 'Is this what you're playing, Bethany?' Beth held her breath. 'Looks complicated.' she said, dropping it down again.

'Careful Mum!'

'Well, I don't know where you get your talent from. Can't be me!' she chuckled. 'Can't sing for toffee,' is what your nan used to say.'

The second she'd left the room, Beth grabbed the music and stared hard at it.

'Four more lines!' she screeched. 'Four lines of pure magic. It worked! It worked!' she exclaimed, bounding from her bed. Beth tried to contain her excitement as she washed and dressed, nearly forgetting her breakfast, before placing her new music on the piano stand. She began patiently working out the new section of music, relying on her aunt's little book and a good dose of determination. 'It's the piece the professor gave me,' smiled Beth as her mum popped her head around the door. 'I'm learning a bit more each week.'

'Well, *you* keep practising, love. I'm sure he'll be very pleased with you. I'll go and see to Ted.'

'Mum, *he's ecstatic!*' declared Beth, turning to her mum.

'Ecstatic, did you say?' she laughed. 'Don't you think that's a bit over the top?'

'Yes, I do!' replied Beth smiling, continuing her practice. Some twenty minutes later, Beth ended with a rapid scale in C major. 'That should do it!' she said, triumphantly and closed the piano lid firmly. 'Done!'

Beth and Ted raced to catch the school bus for the last time before the long summer break.

'Just two more lessons with the professor, Beth, then we'll be off to visit Aunt Alice,' announced Beth's mum on their return from school. 'I told her how well you're playing now. She says she can't *wait* to hear you play her piano.'

'Great!' smiled Beth broadly, happy with this especially good news. 'There'll be time for making more musical magic before our visit,' she thought, 'more piano playing once there, *and* time with Aunt Alice. Great!'

Ted, on the other hand, groaned.

'What's up with you, Ted?' asked his mum.

'Aunty Alice is just *so fussy* all the time,' he said, slumping on the settee.

'Really? I think it's just that she doesn't see you as often as she'd like, that's all.... And, living on her own she's used to keeping the place tidy.'

'She *is* a bit posh though, Mum,' added Beth, in his defence.

'Well, so what? She is the way she is, and that's that. Right! Who's for spag bol tonight?'

Beth's mum disappeared to the kitchen to a resounding '*meeee*!' from both Ted and Beth.

Until recently, Beth had played the piano just as and when she felt like it. But now she felt a sense of achievement and the possibility of getting so much better, that she practised every day. During lessons she would play her best, impressing her professor and leaving with the special gift of more musical notes. They transformed in the night into all manner of notes, just as Beth had hoped and wished.

'It's like I'm *growing* music!' Beth laughed, one morning.

But her curiosity was deepening. She wanted to know the name of the piece, who composed it, and more especially *why she* had been given the notes. She planned to ask the professor at her next lesson, the last one before September. As it turned out she completely forgot to ask him, having been swept up with his growing enthusiasm for her playing.

'Remember Beth, it's about progress, not perfection,' he told her. 'Enjoy yourself and keep going! You'll have a *wonderful* summer!'

Beth, Ted and their mum spent nearly three weeks at the home of Aunt Alice. For her aunt, it was a big change from her usual ritual of taking tea and running the village quiz nights with her spinster friends. Nevertheless, she seemed to relish the opportunity to lavish her affection towards her niece and nephew. When it became a bit too much, Ted would excuse himself and be found later buried in a pile of comics or picking blackberries from heaving brambles. Sometimes, Beth would join him, finding ways to pass the time exploring local woodland together, or making strawberry milkshakes to approving looks from their mum. Alice always made sure she had a plentiful supply of the best organic vanilla ice cream for their visits.

Beth was happy to spend a lot of the time playing her music, practising her pieces and scales and enjoying the attention from her aunt and mum. Ted tried to compete with his batman impersonations, much to the amusement of all.

'You're making *super* music Bethany, darling.' said her aunt. 'That piece sounds strangely familiar. What is it?'

'I don't know yet. I mean, I don't know!' replied Beth more carefully. 'But do you *really* think you might have heard it before?'

'Um ... possibly ... though I don't seem to remember the name...anyway, you're playing it beautifully,' she said, peering close. 'I'm afraid I don't play so much now. Anyway, don't let me stop you,' said Alice, tiptoeing away.

Long days ran into over two weeks. Beth kept up her piano practice and persuaded her aunt to play the piano pieces she could remember. Ted ran out of comics and games and began to feel bored, and their mum seemed to run out of conversation with Aunt Alice. It was time to go home.

'Seeuw-pah,' teased Ted on their journey home.

Beth was used to her brother's humour and smiled. Her mum laughed.

'Actually, that sounded *just* like your aunt!' she laughed.

Beth thought the break must have done her mum good. Once home, she watched her unpack all the bags and begin gathering the laundry into piles on the landing. Beth slumped against the banister and gazed thoughtfully.

'Do I *have* to go back to school?'

'Of course you do, silly Billy! Why, what's the matter?'

'I just *don*'t like it, that's all. Those girls….' she began.

'You'll be alright, love. Just stay away from those *petty* girls and bury your nose in your books.'

Beth didn't want to stay away from them or bury herself in books. She ran her hand up and down the wooden banister until her palm began to squeak.

'What day is it?' she asked.

'Monday! Why, love?'

Beth had already headed down the stairs, before making a U-turn to pick up the laundry basket and carry it down for her mum.

'Thank you, honey,' she called.

Beth checked the kitchen calendar. It read **Thursday 4th September 4.30pm Professor Rubato.**

'Rubato, Rubato. Wonder if that means something,' she said.

Thursday came at last. Professor Rubato's welcoming smile put Beth at ease after the long summer break.

'I expect you've been working hard with your music, huh?'

'Yes, I have, Professor,' she replied, striding confidently towards the vacant stool. 'I hope it sounds okay.'

'I'm sure you needn't worry, Beth. It'll *all* make sense, I assure you. How was your holiday?' Beth had already opened the page. 'Oh, so then er … how far have you got with it?' he asked.

Beth gave no reply but began to play her scales, launching straight into playing C major.

'Strikes me, you *have* been working hard. That was very well played. And how is the *new* piece going? Let's hear that, if you will?' The professor leaned in, poised to listen. Beth began keenly. She took extra care with the tricky parts, slowing to get her fingering right, yet trying to keep the sound lively. When she had finished all that she could play, there was an unexpected silence. Beth turned slowly to face him, sweeping her fringe from her face.

'I *knew* this moment would come,' he said, leaning back and inhaling deeply…

'And *you* have shown the commitment needed for the next …'

'For the next *grade, really? Already*?' she said, cutting in.

But the professor seemed to be running through a list in his head, counting and mumbling incoherently.

'So, I played it okay?' she persisted.

'Okay. *Okay?*' he repeated louder. 'You played *brilliantly*, Beth! I mean, there are some parts that need a little more attention,' he said, fumbling with his pocket watch, 'but nothing that can't be sorted with a little more work and … and …'

'And?' urged Beth.

'And adventure!' he cheered, shooting unexpectedly from his chair and swinging around to face her. 'But I'll need you to map read, Beth.'

'*Map* read? Where are we going?' she replied, bewildered.

He gestured her to stand up. Beth moved aside. The professor lifted the lid of the stool and picked out a small booklet from inside. He was beaming.

'For the navigator,' he announced, proudly presenting it to Beth.

She held the booklet in front of her then looked blankly at him. The words on its cover read 'Flight Manual'.

'But this is a … Flight Manual?' she said, handing it back.

'That's it. *That's the one!*' he replied instantly.

Tucked away in the corner of the room was a large, double piano stool, covered with stacks of old music. The professor began clearing it speedily.

'Can I help?' said Beth, pushing up her sleeves keenly? 'Are we going to *duet*, Professor?'

He passed her a smallish pile to move with the other stool. '*This* one will serve us better,' he grinned as they carried it over, positioning it in place of the old stool.

'Come, take your seat.'

He closed the piano top, gently lying flat the supporting stick. Next, using a cherry red handkerchief, he buffed the ebony surfaces to a shine and stood back to admire his work. 'All present and correct,' he smiled, patting his jacket pockets. Next, he removed a small red box from behind a china figurine and retrieved something from inside it. 'I've waited so long for this,' he said, stretching out his hand to reveal a tiny silver key.

Beth was intrigued.

'How has a key got anything to do with learning a duet?' she thought.

'Please hold this,' he said, passing her the metronome.

She placed it on her lap. But it was when he took the golden manuscript and pressed open the first blank page that she began to feel her heart race. It was glowing fiercely.

'What's happening?' she mouthed as he laid the silver key on top.

Placing the open manuscript beside her, he then stood back. Beth's eyes widened as notes slowly began to appear onto the page, creating a short untitled piece of music. He looked at the page carefully then lifted it onto the stand to show Beth. Before she could utter a word, he began to play it.

'I knew it!' she thought, giving him some elbow-room. 'He's a magician!'

The last note had a pause sign. When he came to it, he held it down.

'What's the time?' he said.

'Huh? The time? Er…' Beth checked her wrist-watch. 'It's ten to five. Why? Do I need to go?'

'Four-fifty? Thank you, Beth. Okay. All that remains now is *the grand charge.*'

'Uh oh,' thought Beth, bracing herself.

But *nothing* could have prepared her for what was about to happen next.

5. Volante

'Allow me!' insisted the professor, shifting into position beside her. He began with four octaves in the keys of A major, C, then E major, playing with escalating volume and intensity. Beth found herself swaying right and left in sync with him as he reached the top and bottom notes of each scale. 'That should do it, Beth.'

Beth looked astonished.

'Comes... with... practice,' he laughed. 'Now .... hold tight. We're all charged and ready... *to go*.'

'Go?' said Beth, standing to attention.

'No, sit, if you will. We're just about ready... *Volante!*' he commanded.

'What? Where?' she snapped.

'*Volante!*' he repeated, stamping his foot.

Nothing seemed to be happening. She pulled her aunt's little book from her pocket. Her hands were shaking in excitement as she flicked from the back page.

'Volante!' she read aloud. 'But... it means... *flying?*'

The professor had moved. He was hastily unbolting the triple doors to the garden patio. He threw them wide open and quickly returned to sit beside her.

'Fancy forgetting about the way out!' he laughed. Situated roughly below the middle C note was a keyhole. He pushed the silver key in and turned it clockwise. It was a little stiff. He tried again. 'Volante!' he called, staring ahead. 'If you will…'

All at once the piano began to shudder. Beth held on to her seat as she, the professor *and* the piano began to turn together, clockwise at first, bearing right a little, forward, looping around at the front window, then straight back along the length of the room, before shooting through the open French doors. 'Just like a horse bolting from the stable!' laughed the professor, clinging to the seat also.

The two bobbed and bounced unceremoniously as the piano juddered and jolted along the garden. Beth wedged the metronome between her knees. Her grip tightened. 'Hold on,' he warned, 'this is the tricky bit. I'll need your help with the launch, Beth,' he shouted. 'Quickly! What does it say to do next? Have you found the page? We mustn't run out of garden! … Beth?'

Beth freed one hand warily and opened the flight manual to the first page. 'Errrrr…' she replied shakily, 'it says '*accel … er … ando*' and… there's a 120bpm, I th… think?'

'That's good, Beth. That's a s..speed of one hu.. hundred and twenty be...beats per minute,' he said, slamming his foot on the forte pedal as she simultaneously saved the metronome from certain misfortune. 'Set the beat mon... monitor to 120!' he commanded.

'120 – check!' she replied, sensibly wrapping her legs around one leg of the stool.

'Hold tight, Beth. *Accelerando*!' he bellowed.

They charged ahead into the narrow garden strip – turned – runway, gathering speed. Very soon they were airborne. As the cooler air hit her face, Beth opened her eyes. She looked back at the remarkable scene they were fast leaving behind, and a trail of golden dust, magically shaped into an *enormous* treble clef.

'Look Professor!' she called, craning her neck.

'Isn't it just wonderful?' he laughed, glancing back.

But Beth's eyes were now tightly shut. She could feel they were gaining height rapidly yet willed them to open. At the sound of three loud clicks, Beth leant cautiously back and saw the piano legs folding tidily beneath its ebony undercarriage. Her fear quickly turned to wonder.

'This is *no dream*,' she said, 'we really *must* be flying now!'

Once they had climbed to a horizontal, Beth sighed in relief. She heard the professor do the same.

'Phew! Now, see over there?' he called, jabbing excitedly at a landmark below.

Beth dared a glimpse at the river weaving through the city.

'I don't feel very well, Professor.'

'Oh? I expect that's the Quaver Quivers!' he replied, making light of the situation. 'I've got *just* the melody for *that* malady!' he chuckled. 'Start with a few deep breaths and....' After playing a few gentle harmonic chords, he smiled reassuringly at Beth. The remedy began to work almost immediately. 'Better?'

'*Much* better, thanks,' she replied, gaining colour.

'Good. Now, we'll need to choose the altitude carefully. Can't have a queasy co-pilot, can we?' he smiled.

His old-fashioned distraction tactics were working, and Beth soon forgot all about her sickness. She studied the page. 'There's an 'eight,' 'v' and an 'a'. What does all *that* mean?'

'Means, I'm afraid we'll have to pitch a little higher, that's all. But you'll be alright, Beth.' Beth had to take his word for it. She held on. 'Let's *go 'glissando!'* he called loudly. Their vehicle climbed steadily to a musical altitude of 8va (15). 'We'll be quite safe here,

Beth,' he smiled, '*and* I'm pleased to see that we seem to have cured your altitude sickness.'Beth nodded. 'So, let's just enjoy the ride.' Beth was glad of his timely reassurance. 'Look back and you can see the meadows,' he said delightedly.

Beth glimpsed over her shoulder at first, then twisted to take a longer look at the vast spread of Grantchester meadows below. The river Cam meandered lazily through its lush greens, disturbed only by a handful of Red Poll cattle.

'It looks beautiful from up here. Where are we going though?' she eventually wondered, searching around the skies.

Ahead and below them, a gentle line of cars and pedestrians edged their way through the city's streets. Any traffic noise was drowned out by the sound of air rushing past their ears.

'*There's* the Mathematical Bridge!' announced the professor. 'See it?'

'So, *that's* Queens' College? she said excitedly, 'with King's over there! It looks *amazing* from up here!'

'You're right!' he laughed, '*Quite* spectacular!'

Beth was enjoying the journey much more, now that she felt less sick and safer than at first. She leaned to the side to get a better view of the punts and canoes

gliding and darting across the river. She waved to the tourists peering endlessly over the ancient bridge, taking photos and licking ice cream.

'Can't they see us, Professor?' she asked, waving harder.

'It appears not,' he replied, skimming over the thirteenth-century Round Church. 'In fact, we could fly *anywhere we want* and not be seen up here,' he chortled.

'Really? So where *are* we going?'

'Oh, not too far, Beth. But you make a very fine co-pilot, you know? Now, are there any more instructions for me?' he asked.

Beth scanned the page, blushing. 'Oh yes. It says '*andante*'.'

'Then *andante it is!*' he laughed, through an uninterrupted expanse of cool blue skies. As their travelling speed steadied over Cambridge, the professor turned to Beth. 'How are you feeling now, hmm?'

'Better thanks,' she smiled.

'So, aren't you going to ask me?'

'Oh, sorry, Professor. Are *you* alright?'

'No. I mean, *yes* I am. I mean, aren't you going to *ask* me? After all, it's rather extraordinary, don't you think?' he chuckled.

'Yes! Well, first, where are we going to, and how did ... and what about my mum and getting home and ... and ... might we crash?' she rushed.

'Steady Beth,' he laughed. 'Listen carefully. Firstly, we're heading to a place not too far from here. A place where dreams *can* come true, believe me.' Beth's eyes widened. 'You *will* be home on time. And *secondly...*' Beth held her breath. 'Yes quite possibly.'

'What, that we might crash?'

The professor cleared his throat. 'Yes, quite possibly.' Beth went rigid. 'But that's *only if* we run out of power. You see it's like any other vehicle. It needs power.'

'Then how do we get it?' she asked, helpfully scanning the terrain below.

'Ah, that's down to you, Beth,' he smiled. 'Do you remember how I played all those scales before we set off?' Beth nodded. 'Well, that was to make the charge that we needed initially – a bit like the battery charge in a car. Do you see?' Beth nodded again. 'The soundboard – that bit running through the middle there,' he pointed, 'is like the heart and soul of the piano,' he explained, 'but it needs vibrational energy to sustain it.' Beth thought she understood, even if it did sound like a school physics lesson. The professor continued. 'Scales *make* this energy, these vibrations. And that's why you *need to know* your scales,' he added. 'This piano needs *you!*'

'So *it's down to me to* keep us up? Up *here?*' she said simply.

'That's it!' he replied calmly. 'Oh, and there's Jesus Green. Look! Now we're heading north of the city.' He paused to take in the view while Beth played his words over in her mind.

'Keep us up here. Scales. Energy. Okay,' she repeated. 'Scales, energy...up!'

'Now just supposing we pitch higher...then we'll need *another* round of scales to get up there.'

'And if we don't?' asked Beth.

'If we don't ...? Then we'll simply ... *diminuendo* from the skies! Do you see?'

Beth could see *exactly* what he meant. '*Diminuendo* from the skies,' she repeated solemnly.

6. Rit, Plop and Tie

The two journeyed ahead. Below them, a colourful sketch of town and field, and the criss-cross of roadways led silent vehicles to their destinations.

'Can I ask something?' said Beth, breaking their quietude.

'Of course, Beth, what is it?'

'Will we be back on time? Mum will be worried.'

The professor answered promptly. 'You've no need to worry about that. We have frozen Time.'

'How? Where?' she said, trying to recall how it worked in the few sci-fi novels she had read.

'Do you remember the 'pause sign' at the end of that piece I played before we left?' Beth nodded unconvincingly. '*That's* the tool I used to put everything on hold, if you like,' he explained, 'giving us *plenty* of time for our adventure. Clever, isn't it?' he chuckled.

Beth thought for a moment then remembered how he had held down the note and asked her the time. 'Yes, it was um … 4.50 *then* … so, is it 4.50 *still?*' she asked.

'Exactly! We'll have you back in no time, you'll see.'

'So, what's next, Professor?' said Beth, seemingly satisfied with his incomplete answer.

'Well, it'll soon be time to receive our first guest!' he announced, rubbing his hands together. 'Let's hope we can find one brave enough to hop on board, shall we? After all, we're going to *need* them,' he chuckled.

'Really? Seriously?' said Beth, puzzling over the prospect.

'Seriously,' said the professor.

Despite these extraordinary circumstances, Beth's flying confidence was growing, and she now thought of her Quaver Quivers as nothing more than the result of a turbulent take off. She squeezed her eyes shut as the occasional cloud enveloped them, leaving a slight dampness on her skin. The professor lifted his foot slightly from the pedal, easing them into a gentle '*legato*' lilt. They smiled at each other as he stretched into a long and contented yawn.

'Know something, Beth? I used to be young like you…full of dreams. But, you see, I wanted it all too quickly – the brilliance of performance – the result! I never used to practise anywhere *near* enough. Do you believe that?' he said.

'Really?' she said, familiar in part with his story.

'What I needed was *inspiration, motivation*, and a *real* passion, *a self-belief* to get to where I wanted – to the top and in charge.'

'What do you mean?'

'I mean, the one pulling the strings and creating something really special, something unique…to be the conductor!' he said emphatically. 'It was only then that I discovered that there was more to it than…than just waving one's arms around,' he said, demonstrating.

Beth giggled.

'You see, the orchestra has to *trust* the conductor. In fact,' he reflected, 'only half my job was conducting, the other was simply managing *people*',

'You're a conductor, too?'

'Indeed, I am. You look surprised Beth.'

'Hmm, perhaps,' she said quizzically.

'I used to be quite fearful of performance,' he said, reading her mind, 'had very little self-belief, I guess.'

'Oh?'

'Until I learnt that *I, too,* could keep an unruly brass band in check, rustle up the woodwind into a *wild* frenzy, the percussion into a passion…. and indeed the beautiful strings… creating a sound altogether *atmospheric!*'

Beth tried to form her reply.

'An optimistic *band of glory!*' he burst out, visibly startling her and making her laugh.

She checked the metronome setting whilst trying to take it all in. So much had happened in such a short space of time.

'All fine,' she reported helpfully.

'That's good,' he said, continuing, 'And the price of making music is in sweat and tears … in hard but *joyful work!* But it's about the *journey you make* as much as the performance. And you, Beth, have an opportunity and a quiet confidence to explore the *wonderful* gamut of musical expression.'

'The what?' she asked softly.

'See, it all starts with a desire,' he said, placing his fist to his chest. Beth turned to face him. He looked both serious and emotional. 'Don't be afraid to create *naturally*. Create from your thoughts, from your heart. Seldom are we *invited* to b*e* creative. Here's *your* chance, Beth. After all, that's why you were put to the test. You have risen to the challenge with interest, belief and commitment.'

Beth stared ahead thoughtfully before finding her words.

'So, *all* this is to do with the crotchets you gave me?'

'Correct,' he said, '*and* of course, your curiosity and determination to learn. After all, music is not music until it is played. You *made* them *come alive*.'

Beth's moment to reply was interrupted by the rapidly approaching sound of an engine.

'Professor!' she burst out, 'I can hear a …'

'I hear it too!' Behind them a light aircraft was closing in on them. '*Attacca! Doppio movimento!*' he shouted.

'*Doppio* – do – what?'

'Double the speed!' he yelled. 'Set the metronome! Hold tight!'

'Done it!' she called, bracing herself.

Moments later, the professor turned around, screwing his face against the rushing air as they hurtled away.

'Are we safe?' Beth called.

'*Seems* so. And *legatissimo please!*' he urged, 'as smoothly as possible, if you will'.

Beth squinted behind to a plane that seemed far from view.

'It's gone!' she sighed as the two listened.

'I think you're right, Beth,' he said, wiping a brow. 'It must have changed altitude, thank goodness. Well done on your skilful negotiation, Beth...Are you okay?'

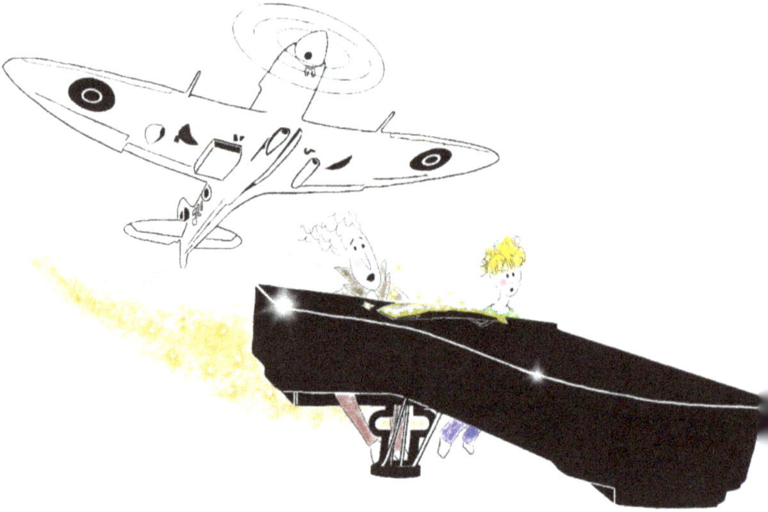

'Just about, I think, thanks,' she said, rechecking her settings.

'Good. Let's *Tempo Rubato*,' he said softly, catching his breath.

'Isn't that like your name…'Rubato?'' she asked, freeing a hand for the metronome.

'Exactly. It means 'in robbed time'. *Tempo* Rubato,' he added – 'with some freedom of time', – gives us a bit of flexibility!'

'All these musical terms! – I didn't know they had *so many* hidden meanings,' laughed Beth, 'let alone *magical powers!'* She recalled the 'pause' sign and felt she now understood how they were able to steal time for their adventure. 'I really hope it works,' she thought, 'after all it's got to be at least half an hour since we left the real world. But then, what is real and what isn't?' she mused.

'Are we on course, Professor?'

'We're doing just fine,' he smiled. 'I was just wondering, Beth, what is your dream, I mean, what would you *really like* to do?'

Beth's answer came quickly. 'I want to be able to do something *really well*…like, piano playing.'

'Oh well, that's…'

''Cos they say I'm not good enough!'

'Do *they?*' he replied gently.

Now Beth felt she had to explain. Her words tumbled out between sniffles. She wondered if their near miss was to blame for her emotions but continued all the same. 'Some girls think I'm stupid, and I don't know how to show them *I'm not.*'

'I see,' he replied, offering a folded handkerchief. 'We'll have to see about that. But there *is one thing* you can do to help. And that's to believe in yourself.' He smiled.

Beth dabbed her tears. 'Thank you,' she muttered, beginning to feel more cheerful.

'Now, we'll soon be approaching McKee's,' said the professor excitedly. 'It's time for our descent, Beth. Do you have the Manual handy? Oh, and the Golden Manuscript? Keep that *especially* safe when we land. It's *most* important!'

Beth's heart leapt at the prospect of landing.

'Descent! '*Glissando,*' she read with no time to think.

'Ready?'

'Ready.'

Beth secured the metronome and clutched her seat as they entered a smooth nosedive. She felt her ears 'pop'. The professor looked keenly around.

'He's here ... somewhere ... *Largo!*' he yelled, spotting something significant.

'*Largo* 40-60 bpm,' read Beth with helpful importance.

'Good. Good. Make it 40-60!' he said, squinting below. Beth freed her sweaty grip and adjusted the settings. 'I can *just* see the church… the park….and… *there* it is!' he shouted excitedly, immediately reaching for his top pocket and pulling out the tuning fork. Beth watched the professor toss it towards a row of cottages edging the town. It spiralled out of sight. 'Should land close enough,' he remarked, appearing chuffed with his aim.

'Close to what?'

'McKee!' he shouted.

'Which one? *Which* key?' she asked, her eyes darting in every direction.

The professor erupted in laughter. 'I mean my *friend*, McKee! He lives in that end house,' he said, pointing to a shabby, off-white terrace. Its long, narrow garden was cluttered with old machinery, broken fencing and a yapping terrier, leaping in restricted spaces.

'Can *he* see us?' asked Beth, mildly amused.

'No. Not until we're on the ground, Beth. Now, let me see…'

'Who *is* he?'

'Our piano tuner!'

'Is he coming with us?'

'Of course, I insist on *the b*est sound. Now we need to turn...just *here*!' he said, jabbing at the Manual.

'*Turn... turn*'... she searched. 'It says '*turn*' then '*trill*'. Their vehicle turned and hovered until in '*trill*' mode, then unexpectedly moved into a shuddering shuffle.

'We're losing charge Beth!' he called. Beth pushed the manual and manuscript into the professor's hand and quickly wedged the metronome again between her knees. She began to play a scale. 'Keep going! *More,* Beth!' The professor meanwhile shifted his feet rapidly between pedals until eventually they lifted and steadied. '*Very* well done! You saved us from another disaster! And you knew *how* to!' he said, recovering from the excitement. 'Now, let's drop anchor here. Read the 'double bar' section, if you will,' he said, handing back the manual.

'Okay. Double bar. '*Rit, plop* and *tie!*' she said. '*Plop?*' she repeated. 'Is there a safety net?'

'No need,' he laughed, calling 'start '*ritardando*,' if you will'. They lowered gracefully to his command over a stretch of open green. 'And now...'*plop!*' he smiled.

The three legs of the landing gear clicked out into position. Beth braced herself for touchdown. After one small jolt they were on the ground, safely cruising into a generous curve to leave the shape of a perfect bass clef, dusted in gold on the flattened grass of their landing strip.

'Wow!' laughed Beth, justifiably triumphant.

'And '*tie*,' he said, giving the final command.

'Care to stretch your legs, Beth?'

'Where are we?' she asked, shuffling off the stool.

'Not entirely sure,' he replied. 'But see that church spire over there and the row of houses? Well, I just headed for *them* and the piano does the rest.'

'How can…?' she began, but the professor was on the move.

7. Welcome Aboard

He leapt off the stool, carefully turning his feet to form two impressions beside the golden curve. 'I get it!' squealed Beth. 'A treble clef at take-off and a bass clef to land!' she giggled.

'*Exactly*!' he laughed.

Beth dismounted carefully, sweeping her hand along the warm ebony piano top. She crouched inquisitively beside the piano and saw brackets secured between criss-crossed wooden strips. She moved right underneath for closer inspection of the landing mechanism.

'Well, Beth? Is she up to any more travel?' called the professor from across the green.

'Huh?' she replied, almost knocking her head.

'I mean, can she make it to our next destination, do you think?'

Beth gasped at the idea of doing it all again.

'Seriously?' she said, turning to him.

Just then a figure approached. He was scruffily dressed and held his head awkwardly for some reason. His purposeful walk led him straight towards the professor and his young companion. They watched his silent, rapid approach. Beth could just make out a patch over his left eye. Moments later he was upon them. In a single deft movement, he drew something from inside

his coat pocket and pointed it at the two. Beth felt a rush of heaviness sink to her legs and ducked instinctively, scrambling to safety and squatting low between the piano legs. Her heart was pounding.

'Pro...fessor?' she croaked; her hands fixed to her ears. 'H... he's got a g…gun.'

Moments later she heard him speak.

'*Come* my friend,' he beckoned cheerfully towards McKee.

Beth opened her eyes to find the two men engaged in friendly conversation. She realised there was nothing sinister after all, as she watched him return the tuning fork to his pocket.

'Oh, I see! *McKee* must have picked it up.'

He spoke. 'McKee's the name. And you're the one, are ya?' Beth nodded nervously as he offered a hurried handshake. 'Aren't you gonna talk?' he said, heading toward the stool.

'This is my friend Beth,' said the professor kindly.

McKee lifted the piano top and inspected the strings and hammers before playing some chords.

'You see how this one got its name? Anyway, altitude affects the tone *real* bad,' he said, turning to the waiting professor.

'Will you do it here McKee?'

'Do what?' Beth asked of the professor.

'Well, tune it of course!' the man boomed in her direction, stabbing at his coat pocket. ''Swat I'm here for!' he said, tut-tutting his way past her.

She realised *that* all too late but resigned herself to talk very little to this rude man, named McKee.

The professor appeared to be carrying out some checks on their vehicle before announcing brightly, 'Now we are *three!* Over to you, Beth!'

'You mean the girl's in charge?' said McKee looking disgruntled and seating himself hesitantly at the end.

Beth inched up her sleeves and passed both booklets directly to the professor.

'So, where to, Professor?' she asked confidently.

'Just airborne, if you will,' he grinned. Beth knew the drill. She played three octaves in two scales with a renewed determination. Her fingers felt warm and energised. She glanced proudly at the professor who returned a beam of approval. 'Pass McKee the metronome, and ... v*olante!*' he called, slamming his foot hard on the pedal. Beth quickly handed it over without looking at him. 'McKee? Metro 160, if you will, please...and...*Accelerando!*' he shouted. They lurched forward, curving in a treble clef before ascending with a 'whoosh' into the waiting skies. Beth was pleased to be airborne again. Her only concern was her new travelling companion. Her thoughts were momentarily interrupted by the professor's next instruction.

'Glissando to 15va.'

'Check,' she said, her hair blowing into the cloudless sky.

Beth realised she still felt all right, no queasy tummy this time. She turned to tell the professor. He seemed to be brimming with excitement.

'Do you realise that this is going to be something *great? Spectacular, in fact!*' he said, bobbing in his seat.

Beth glanced at McKee. He remained silent, nodding and grinning.

'Whatever do *they* know that I don't?' thought Beth nervously. Her wristwatch read 4.50pm. She tapped it. 'Ah, the frozen time thing!' she remembered. 'Professor, the 'pause' really seems to work!' she said, delighted. 'Are we getting close now?'

'You'll recognise it when we're there,' he replied simply. Beth leaned in, hoping for clues, as the professor thumbed through several pages of the Golden Manuscript. He stopped to scrutinise one page. She felt a rush of excitement. 'I wonder if these notes have the same magical powers as those I took home …'

Suddenly the professor called out, 'A trombonist! I need a trombonist!' Beth was startled. McKee laughed huskily. 'We *must* have one,' the professor repeated.

'Whatever *next?*' thought Beth, before suddenly remembering the boy at school who played one. He got mocked for being overweight. Toby was his name, but everyone called him 'Tubby Toby,' though not usually to his face.

'You're quiet Beth. Know any trombonists?' asked the professor.

'Well, I do,' she muttered half-heartedly, 'but I …'

'Well, *take* me to him, if you will.'

'It's just that …' she began.

'What Beth?'

'I don't mean to be rude, but he's a bit on the *large* side. There'll be no room! That is, if you were thinking of picking *him* up too?'

'Oh, is that *all*?' he replied, unintentionally leaving Beth embarrassed.

'I know where he lives!' she gushed helpfully.

'Good. Then close your eyes and imagine the address, if you will.'

'Ooh, more magic,' she thought, smiling and screwing her eyelids shut. She could remember the front door clearly. After all, it was the house where she was born. Toby's parents had bought it when she, Ted and her mum had moved out. 'Number 12!' she announced, almost immediately, 'and it's called Tara.' Before too long a black number 12 appeared in the fuzziness and just below it a small wooden plaque with 'Tara' etched on its faded front. 'I see it! I see it!' she screeched.

The professor was urging her. 'Go on. Knock. *Knock hard!*'

Beth knocked forcefully into the airspace and opened her eyes. Incredibly, her hand was gripped around the brass door knocker as she found herself standing in front. She dropped it in shock, making a resounding thud.

Seconds later, Toby appeared in the open doorway, clutching a packet of pickled onion crisps. They both froze. Beside the thought 'it's impossible', Beth could find no words. But she could feel the gravel path beneath her feet and smiled awkwardly before turning to the professor, parked at the top of the path. He seemed to be beckoning them over.

12
Tara
Pickled

'Er … hop aboard!' she said, as if this was normal. 'Oh, and bring your crisps! Er… and your trombone!' she laughed. Remarkably, moments later, thirteen-year-old Toby had squeezed in beside Beth with his trombone held firmly on his lap. They were swept up and away immediately, as if on autopilot. It was a few minutes before the unsuspecting trombonist found his voice and elbowed Beth in her side. 'Ouch! What was that for?' she asked indignantly.

'Well, you got me up here. Now, what is *going on?* I wanna get down!' he yelled rudely.

'Wait, Toby,' she said, rubbing her side, 'stop shouting! We're on an adventure, can't you see?'

'What's it got to do with me?' he shouted, snorting into his crisp packet. 'And you want me to play my trombone, too, I suppose?' he snorted.

'It depends if you're any good. Are you?' asked the professor.

Toby grunted.

'You know, it's all a bit of a mystery to me, too,' Beth said gently. 'Why don't you just sit back and enjoy the ride? You can always ask the professor about it, you know? After all, it's *his* piano and *he's* in charge, … there *is a bit* of magic going on though,' she warned helpfully.

'You don't say!' replied Toby.

Beth silenced herself at his response and tried to figure out how they'd arrived at his house. 'Was it me or the piano?' she asked, puzzling quietly. 'Me or …' she said.

Toby interrupted. 'What are you talking about?' he asked impatiently.

Beth threw a nod towards the professor.

'Thank you for joining us, Toby,' the professor said, sensing rising tension, 'allow me to introduce myself as Professor Rubato, and … the very able, Mr McKee'.

Toby smirked. 'So, Mr Professor,' he said, fidgeting in his seat and causing mild turbulence, 'you can take me back immediately!' he demanded. '*Please!*'

'Look, young man, Toby, I'm sorry for the inconvenience and all of that,' he said, calmly readjusting the flight mode settings, 'but it seems we *need you*. Why, you *like* music, don't you?' Toby nodded almost imperceptibly, nervous of commitment. 'Well, I, … sorry, *we,*' the professor continued, pointing to his travelling companions, 'are giving you the chance to see the bigger picture. See?'

Beth suddenly recalled her earlier conversation with the professor and felt a flash of insight. She listened hard.

'But *first*, Toby,' he said, 'I need to hear your scales, if you will?'

Toby looked aghast. *'My scales! Up here?'*

'Why ever not?' teased the professor. 'You *can* play them sitting down, can't you?' he smiled. 'If you'd be so kind…'

Beth looked at him and nodded encouragingly. Toby had a change of heart and shifted as far back as he dared, his generous behind having already claimed more than his fair share of the seat. He pressed the mouthpiece to his lips and blew. He tried again, blowing harder and pushing the slide further away as each note sounded. As he climbed the scales the sound disappeared fast from the flared bell, passing the attuned ears of the professor, who sat poised for musical accuracy. When he finished, the professor broke into applause.

'Enough indeed!' he clapped, 'a dedicated *musician, I see you are*! Welcome aboard!'

Toby's cheeks flushed. 'Musician?' he smiled, 'no one's ever called me *that* before! Thanks!'

Beth joined in their applause. McKee looked suitably impressed, but said no more than, 'good, quite good.'

8. 'Swing boy, swing!'

'Tell you what,' said Toby, 'if I move up on top of this, I'll get more room to play, and you won't have to sit so close to *him!*'

'You mean up *there?* What? Hang on, Toby, you know McKee?' she whispered.

'Yeah, he's *bad* news.'

'What? Really? Why?'

'We all heard about it eventually. And Mum wouldn't have him back to tune our piano after that.'

'Shhh,' said Beth nervously. 'What's he done?'

'See, what happened was, he was on this job,' continued Toby keenly, 'took his crowbar to force entry into some house and it slipped, didn't it? Flicked back straight into his eye.'

Beth winced.

'Went straight through the middle, didn't it, turning it into a *real mush.*' he said grinning.

'Gory or *what?*' said Beth in a low voice.

'So, he trailed blood *all the way* to the hospital, wriggling and squealing, and needed an operation to *gouge* his eye out.'

'Oh, stop it! *Please!*' implored Beth holding her middle.

'Called an enu – cle – ation or something.' he added smugly.

'What are you two chatting about?' enquired the professor suddenly.

'Oh! Um … Toby was just telling me all about piano tuning,' said Beth hastily.

'How interesting,' he replied.

McKee turned his head slowly towards them, saying nothing.

'So can he see?' she asked.

''Course he can, with the *other* eye.'

'Was he caught?'

'Yeah, and punished, too.'

'Wow!' said Beth, her eyes widening.

'When he gets his false eye, he can get rid of that patch. Wouldn't trust him though, one *or* two-eyed,' he sniggered.

The professor cleared his throat. Beth said no more. She didn't know whether to believe Toby, despite his ghoulish detail, but agreed to help him to get away from McKee.

'Wait,' she said, 'you'd better ask Professor first'.

Toby explained to the professor that there'd be more comfort for them all if he moved on top of the piano.

The professor joked. 'You *do* realise I'll have to charge you first class travel rates?'

McKee stifled a smile.

'Here. Hold this, would you?' said Toby, thrusting the trombone at Beth whilst closing the lid over the keys to form a temporary step. The professor offered him a steadying hand as he balanced a foot precariously on the lid and reached across the breadth of the piano top.

'Careful!' shouted McKee. 'Easy does it, Toby, *now* turn. That's it!'

The professor took charge of the flight settings throughout, while Toby manoeuvred himself into a backward facing, cross-legged position. Beth helpfully tried to rub off the marks from Toby's trainers, which had left short streaks on the polished ebony. The professor discreetly handed a handkerchief to her from the colourful collection kept in his jacket pocket. McKee opened the lid again.

'Nope. Can't do this. Feel sick!' said Toby almost immediately, attempting to turn around. He lifted his feet clear and pushed himself into a slow swivel. In seconds his weight had shifted to one side, throwing the piano off balance. Toby was now dangerously close to the edge.

'Hold on, boy!' yelled the professor, instinctively slamming down his foot.

McKee lunged forward to grab Toby. Beth screamed. Toby slid clear off the edge.

The once calm skies now spoke of panic and confusion. McKee snatched the trombone from Beth and dismantled the well-greased slide. He jabbed it repeatedly at the air below.

Luckily, Toby was dangling from something underneath and grabbed hold of it just in time.

'Hang on! I'll get you up!' hollered McKee, executing an impromptu rescue plan.

Toby, of course had no choice but to hang on. McKee anchored his legs tightly around the piano stool and pulled up hard on the slide brace. Toby clung on to the brassy u-bend with one hand and stretched out his fingertips towards McKee.

'Can't reach! *Help meeee!*'

'Come on McKee. Save the lad!' called the professor unhelpfully.

'Swing, boy. *Swing!*' shouted McKee.

Toby began to swing his legs, gathering enough momentum to eventually reach higher. McKee leaned as low as he could, his hand outstretched. After a few attempts they made contact.

'Gotcha!' he called.

McKee grabbed Toby by the arm and, mustering all his strength, pulled him up.

Toby clambered onto the padded seat beside him.

'Not… such… a… good idea… after all!' he puffed, tucking in his shirt and staring below.

McKee was nursing his neck and arm and shook his head.

'Are you alright, Toby?' burst out the professor sympathetically.

'I'm okay, I think, … thanks to *Mr* McKee!'

'And I reckon I've got one arm longer than the other *now!*' McKee joked. 'Least the lad's safe,' he added, rubbing feeling into his legs.

No one spoke for several seconds. Toby sat giggling awkwardly before offering a sudden handshake to McKee. 'Want some?' he said, yanking the half full packet of crisps from his pocket.

Mr McKee peered into the crumbs and shook his head, giving Toby a friendly slap on his back. Toby scoffed the rest and tossed the packet into the under-currents.

Beth tutted. 'That's not helping the environment!'

'Oh, *please!* I could've nearly *died!*'

Mr McKee handed him back the trombone parts, inspecting them as he did so. As Toby reassembled the instrument, he noticed some distortion of the metal and discoloration on the u-bend where the lacquer had worn off.

'That'll fix,' said McKee.

'Not too worried about that,' said Toby, his cheeks pink and hair wild, 'it … and *You* … saved my life!'

Beth squeezed Toby's arm briefly and smiled.

'Good to have you back, Toby,' said the professor, leaning behind Beth. 'Oh, and never judge a book by its cover.' He winked. 'Now Beth, let's *allegro ma non troppo!* Oh, and there'll be no overtaking on a blind bend,' he teased.

'Are we nearly there?' asked Toby.

'You sound just like my brother on a long car journey!' Beth laughed.

Professor Rubato joined in. 'Actually, we're not far at all, but there's one more passenger waiting.'

McKee detected a certain tone in his voice. 'Anyone in partic'lar?' he said, clearly teasing the professor.

'Someone quite partic'lar!' laughed the professor. 'Her name is Ruth.'

Toby nudged Beth. 'Hope she plays the piccolo, 'cos there's not much room for anything else up here!'

Beth laughed and so did the professor.

'*Allegro!*' he called, peering below. 'Now, let me see. Splendid. We're in Fulbourn already!' said the professor.

Beth skilfully negotiated their way past the village windmill.

'What are we looking for?' asked Toby.

A glint from something flashed towards them, like a signal.

'Over there!' they shouted together.

'*Glissando* to *8va*!' commanded the professor. 'Closer!'

'You'll skim the rooftops if we go any lower,' warned McKee.

'*Un ... be ... lieveable!*' said Toby squinting at it.

'What?' said Beth, twisting on her seat.

'Look *there!*' replied Toby sharply.

'Can't!' replied Beth concentrating.

He was pointing towards a small, thatched cottage, surrounded by open fields. In the cottage garden stood a petite figure angling something large and shiny at them. The professor began waving excitedly. They could just make out a large, flared bell.

Toby was the first to speak. 'You *must* be joking! A French horn, up *here?*'

The professor chuckled. 'Oh, you'll be surprised,' he said.

Beth followed strict landing procedures, safely steering their vessel into a quiet country lane.

'Just pop her down here,' the professor added, smiling broadly.

Mr McKee remained in his seat while the others disembarked. Beth followed Toby.

'Phew!' said Beth, modestly recovering from co-piloting duties. 'Who do you think it is?'

'Dunno!' replied Toby, 'But seems *he* does!'

Just then they heard the professor.

'Ruth? Over here!'

Toby and Beth turned quickly. A woman approached carrying her brassy instrument. As she lifted it playfully to sound some notes, Beth jumped with surprise.

'I know that! And I know *her!'* she said excitedly.

'Miss Ingle!' they shrieked at the same time.

'Well, what's *she* doing here?' said Toby. 'You mean, our teacher's in on this too? And what did she just play?'

'Oh, it's something I've been learning at home,' replied Beth shyly.

Miss Ingle lowered her instrument and greeted the professor with a kiss on his cheek.

'Huh? You're telling me she plays the French horn?'

'I didn't know that either!' exploded Beth, turning to visualise a new seating arrangement.

'What are you two conjuring?' asked the professor, drawing closer.

'Oh Professor,' said Miss Ingle, 'I think it's *you* who does the *best* conjuring,' she laughed.

Beth and Toby stood to attention.

'Hello, you two lovelies of Kingsley High! We're in for a treat and I *can't wait, can you?*'

'Did you see that?' whispered Beth, giggling.

'What?' replied Toby.

'The way she fluttered her eyelashes at him?'

'Oh, leave it out!' sighed Toby.

Mr McKee stood to greet Miss Ingle. 'Ow do, lady!' he said.

'Charmed as always,' replied Ruth, smiling.

'Right,' said the professor, taking charge, 'Let's sort out the seating, shall we?

McKee, will you . . .?'

'Yeh, I know.... *I'll* do it. What's life without a few risks, huh?'

Beth and Toby watched as McKee mounted the piano.

'Sure you wanna do that?' asked Toby.

'No problem,' said Mr McKee, settling himself into a forward-facing position on top of the piano, his knees bent up in front and arms wrapped tightly around them. A gaping hole appeared in the armpit of his coat, having probably ripped it during the rescue.

'Where do you want *us?*' asked Toby brightly.

'Toby, you sit at the end there on the left, if you will. Beth, you go next and then I can accompany you on the keys. Ruth, come to this end here, please,' he smiled, patting the free seat next to him.

Toby turned to Beth, 'Actually, I think they go well together'.

'Robin and Ruth?' giggled Beth.

'No, Miss Ingle and *the French horn*, you muppet!' said Toby, nudging Beth. Beth laughed.

Miss Ingle smoothed over her large blob of iron-grey hair and tightened some pins. Then she cradled the horn in both arms. Beth and Toby looked on.

'Don't you think it's *a bit* strange that *neither of them* seems a jot surprised by all this?' whispered Beth.

'Yeah. I know what you mean. All this flying around and landing,' said Toby, 'it's like they do this every day!'

The professor cleared his throat loudly. 'We're on our way!' he said cheerfully.

'But where to?' asked Toby.

'To a place where dreams come true, *of course,*' laughed Beth.

'You'd believe anything.'

'Oh yeah? Wait and see,' she smiled mischievously. 'But it's true,' she thought, remembering what the professor had told her.

'Over to you, Beth,' smiled the professor, closing the Flight Manual assertively.

'McKee?' he called, 'hold *very* tight!'

McKee gripped on to one side, while his other hand fumbled behind to grasp anything it could and found the opposite edge. Beth then began to power ahead with her scales, earning looks of approval from all parties. She nodded happily, then prompted the professor.

'Volante!' he commanded. There were sighs of relief among the crew as they completed their take-off safely and took to the skies once again.

'Let *me* do the next one!' pleaded Toby, watching closely. Soon after take-off Beth adjusted to cruise mode, combined with another *legato* lilt.

'How do y'know how to do all that?'

'I'm in training,' she smiled.

'Beth's becoming quite the seasoned traveller now, you know,' teased the professor.

'Any more of those Quaver Quivers?'

'Not one!' answered Beth proudly.

'Quaver Quivers!' huffed Toby.

9. Setting the Stage

Throughout this short leg of their journey Miss Ingle and the professor chatted to each other, laughing at times and pointing to various buildings. Beth and Toby talked, between piloting duties, about their summer holidays. Mr McKee stayed fixed to the 'top seat', with his back to the others, until now, turning to alert them to their imminent landing site. Toby and Beth looked at each other in utter disbelief as they began their descent to a surprisingly familiar destination. The grand piano slowed and shuddered safely, curving to a halt on the school grounds of Kingsley High. Mr McKee jumped off with some precision.

'And *tie* … Splendid, Beth. Thank you,' said the professor.

'Are you alright, Miss Ingle?' asked Beth, noting her silence.

'Oh, just a touch of Quaver Quivers. I shall be all right in a minute,' she said, inhaling deeply.

The professor offered to carry her instrument and escorted her the short distance to the rear entrance of the building, leaving Toby and Beth to follow.

'Wait a minute,' grumbled Toby, 'but this is our school playing field! I could have caught the bus!'

'Perhaps we're picking up someone else,' said Beth, propelling herself off the stool.

'All that flying fuss, and musical talk, *and danger*, … and we end up *here!*' he said, lumbering off.

Mr McKee chuckled. 'Just be patient, Toby. You'll see.'

'See what?'

'The professor *promised*,' said Beth quietly. 'He's coming back. Quick!'

'Come along you two, if you will,' he said brightly.

Toby grumbled. 'Why didn't we. . ?' he started.

'In life, it's about the journey,' said the professor kindly, 'not the destination.' Toby had to think about that. Beth thought she understood. 'Right. I'll need you to help me get this inside, if you will.'

'About the journey not the . . .' Toby repeated slowly. 'b … but there's *already one inside*, Professor!' he called. Beth glared at him. 'Can't you just do your magic thing and get it through the roof or something?' the boy asked.

Beth laughed. 'Come on,' she said.

'We don't want to make a fuss now, hmm?' said the professor, 'there's a good chap'.

'Where's Mr McKee anyway?' asked Toby.

'He's inside getting ready, I expect, tuning the other one.' Toby laid his trombone on the piano top and began turning and pulling. Beth helped. The professor steered at the other end and pushed it towards the ramp behind the school hall. Then the three heaved it up the ramp and onto the stage in one go. 'Sterling job you two! Well done! Let's park it over here,' he puffed, indicating the precise spot with his foot and giving them the benefit of his vibrant socks. Toby and Beth giggled as they parked it on the front side of the empty stage. The sound of someone whistling drew closer as Mr Arnold, the evening School Caretaker, leapt onto the stage. He propped up his broom, unclipped the heavy ring of keys from his grey cotton overall, and selected one long key. After unlocking the double doors to the stage cupboard, he turned to them.

'Welcome, Mr Professor,' he called in a voice almost too strong for his size, 'and to you lovely young ones! Must get on,' he said, jumping down the short flight of steps into the hall. He began lifting the chairs from their stacks and arranging them into neat, curved rows.

'What's happening here?' asked Beth.

'You'll see,' smiled the professor, joining Mr McKee by the open stage cupboard.

Together they pulled out the school's old grand piano. Mr McKee had the tuning fork gripped between his teeth as they wheeled it carefully beside the professor's piano.

'What *is* going on?' said Toby impatiently.

'Let's have a little quiet now as we let Mr McKee start his work. Hmm?'

Mr McKee emerged with a handful of tools and lifted the lid of the school piano. Toby broke the silence.

'Why *two* pianos?' he asked.

'Shhh,' frowned Beth.

'So bossy!' he mumbled. Miss Ingle appeared, her hair reformed into a tidy bun and wearing lipstick.

'Just when all the hard work is over, she appears!'

'Shhh, don't be mean,' said Beth, interrupting him mid-grumble. 'Maybe she's saving her energy. It must take *some puff* to play *that* instrument! Anyway Toby, *you* should know.'

Mr McKee was moving between pianos, tightening and adjusting, listening, and sounding keys repeatedly. Beth found Professor Rubato in the recess of the cupboard, dusting off some music sheets. She sneezed loudly. A ripple of laughter followed.

'Oh, my minims and melodies, *bless you!*' he chuckled.

Beth laughed, 'Thank you.'

'Perhaps you'll take these for me?' he said, passing her a pile of manuscripts.

'And *these* are for Ru… er *Miss Ingle*, if you will.'

Beth took them straight to her.

'Thank you, Beth,' she said, 'and, thanks to you and the professor for joining my practice today, and Toby, of course. You'll have a wonderful time!'

Mr Arnold had almost finished putting out the stands as Miss Ingle began distributing the music sheets among them. Beth smiled and returned to her seat with the manuscripts to pick her way through. She found that most of the front covers were missing. But there was one with a cover, torn and folded. She carefully pieced it together to reveal the words 'Brahms. *Allegretto grazioso.* Fourth Movement.' Beth looked up at the professor. He was smiling at her.

'And you'll need this,' he said, beaming as he placed the Golden Manuscript on top.

'Wow!' said Beth, staring at the embossed treble clef. It was sparkling even more brightly.

'This is it! *This is it!*' he danced.

Beth had seen him do this before. 'Professor?' she said simply.

'Come. Sit at my piano. Play what you see. Play your heart away and join in with the others.'

'Others? What others? Play this? What, now?' she said, flicking through.

'Very soon, Beth. You *shall.*'

Beth followed him to the piano, puzzled. She saw the tuning fork resting on the music stand.

'Where's Mr McKee?' she asked.

'Oh, I expect he's finished his work and will be on his way,' he replied, placing her music on the stand.

Beth stared at the music sheet and looked around her. Mr Arnold had finished putting out the music stands between rows of chairs. At the side of the hall, Toby was quietly inspecting the damage to his trombone. He looked up as the professor approached him.

'Toby, we're expecting company. More musicians. Some dedicated and hard working, others with only a fragile belief in their talents, and some needing an *extraordinary* touch of *magic to inspire*. A mix, and *all here* to explore the *wonderful* gamut of musical expression.' Toby shot a glance at Beth, who shrugged her shoulders. 'Here to flex our instrumental muscles!' he added, patting Toby on the back.

'What do I have to do?' Toby asked nervously.

'Just enjoy yourself. Listen, play and you'll *love* the sound!' he said, weaving a paper copy of the trombone part into his hand.

The professor left him and sat beside Miss Ingle. They quickly engaged in conversation. Toby read out the words 'Fourth Movement, Brahms Piano Concerto No. 2 in B flat major,' then opened the first page. He immediately stood up and waved his copy at the professor.

'This is too hard! I've got the wrong one, Professor!' he said, making his way over. The professor directed him back to his seat. Toby dragged his feet. 'Well, I'll just sit this one out!' he moped, until the arrival of a young girl caught his attention. Jess Yates, the girl in the year above him, entered, chatting loudly with her companions. She was carrying an instrument and made for the chair beside him.

'You play trombone too, Tobes?' she said, 'and is *this* what you're playing?' she asked, grabbing the music from his stand.

'Well, er … actually … why, aren't *you, too?*' he laughed awkwardly.

Jess took the sheet from the next stand. 'It looks the same, but . . .'

Toby flicked through his copy then began fidgeting with the slide brace. 'Can't believe she's talking to me,' he mumbled, trying to look calm. '*And* she called me Tobes!'

Jess began buffing the brass bell of her instrument with her sleeve. She was looking straight at him. 'So, when did *you* join the orchestra?' she asked.

'Oh, er.... just now?' he replied, shakily. 'You?'

'Feels like forever!' she laughed, smoothing her long, fair hair, 'but its good fun though.' Jess noticed Beth sitting at the piano. 'Who's the new girl?' she asked.

'Oh, that's just Beth, ... I think.'

Beth was turning pages with slow deliberation.

'Not Beth Bristow?' said Jess, looking again. '*She* won't be able to play here, I mean, not with *us*.'

'Why not? She's *good,* you know. Well, I *think* she is,' he added awkwardly.

A sudden rush of activity followed as more players arrived. Miss Ingle introduced them to the professor, who greeted each one warmly. Instruments of all shapes and sizes were carefully lifted from their cases as the players found their seats. For most, this was their first introduction to the professor and a wave of excitement and anticipation began to fill the school hall.

10. Taking the Baton

'So, what are we doing *today?*' asked Jess enthusiastically, reaching for the music sheets.

'Flexing our instrumental muscles, didn't you know?' laughed Toby, weightlifting his trombone.

Jess giggled. Meanwhile, on the stage, Beth seemed to be puzzling over something.

'Piano 2,' she read. 'So, if I'm 2, *who* is 1?' she said, searching keenly across the knot of bodies gathered for practice. She noticed Jess and frowned. A whistling interrupted her as Mr Arnold leapt onto the stage again, carrying his broom. Beth smiled and watched him disappear into the cupboard. '*This* is the piece I've been learning! *I know this!*' she exclaimed, flicking through the first pages. 'Oh, ... but it gets harder,' she sighed. 'I don't think I...'

'Surprise!' burst an unfamiliar voice. 'Arnold's the name, but you can call me Clarence,' said the caretaker, exercising his finger joints, and perching on the other stool.

'Is *he* really going to...' Beth wondered.

In that instant, Mr Arnold began playing some arpeggios, then some chords. He stopped, looked across and joined her.

'May I?' he smiled, lifting the music from her stand.

'Do you know it?' she asked.

'Oh yes, yes, I do...but I've never played it before,' he said, returning it to her.

'Can you help me? I don't think I can play *it all,*' she said, despondently.

'Oh, but you *will!*' he chuckled, turning away.

Beth stared at the piano keys, unsure what to do. She looked up. Mr Arnold was already sitting at the piano opposite and beaming at her reassuringly. Suddenly the baton sounded authoritatively from the conductor's stand, where the professor was standing tall. Beth shut her eyes.

'*Welcome!* Welcome to *all of you!*' he boomed, tapping the baton three times.

'You are now in *Rubato's time!*'

Beth opened her eyes and let out an instant sigh. 'The magic will save me,' she grinned, really hoping that she was right.

Mr Arnold was still smiling, as was the professor. The players shuffled in their seats, looking confused. Miss Ingle's attentiveness stood out among them. The professor swept his baton across from left to right before spinning around to the two pianists and back again. The players *instantly* sat bolt upright, wide-eyed and poised for play.

'Listen carefully,' he said, clearing his throat. 'You have before you a piece of music created by one of the greatest composers. His name is Johannes Brahms. His work is adventurous, brilliant in its harmony and...'

A violinist interrupted. 'But, Mr Professor, er, Sir.... we don't *know* this one.'

'It's too hard!' said another.

The professor left his podium and continued talking with energy and excitement. 'You *all* have the talent,' he smiled, looking across to Miss Ingle. 'Your teacher knows you well. But you can all try harder... much harder, and Brahms's music will *inspire*. I invite you to breathe life into your precious instruments, *here and now*. Let your musical education take flight as we play this *together!*' he said, striding among them. The players looked at one another. They were speechless, Beth too. By the time he had returned to the stage he had gathered pace and was spinning like a top. The players gasped in disbelief. 'And here's his Fourth Movement of the *wonderful* Piano Concerto Number

2 in B flat major,' he announced shakily, recovering his balance. The hall erupted into laughter.

'Are you a wizard?' asked someone.

'A magician?' said another.

'He's definitely *something!*' said Toby, nodding hard.

Beth listened keenly to their comments. She grinned at the professor as he turned to face the stage.

'See here. We have not one, but two pianos…' he said.

'Yep?' smirked Toby.

Mr Arnold looked up. Beth gasped. The professor looked serious now.

'The *greatest* athletes of *all* instruments, able to compete with courage and confidence!' he continued. 'And today, my young friend, Beth, will join us all in recreating *the musical magic.*'

'I will?' thought Beth. 'If the professor believes in me, then I *will,*' she nodded.

'Will she?' whispered Jess, nudging Toby.

'Guess so!' he shrugged.

'We'll take a moment before we start,' said the professor.

Beth looked across the hall. Two girl flautists huddled together, giggling behind their music stands with faces flushed in excitement. The oboists and clarinettists sat poised for play. She saw Miss Ingle among the other brass players calmly pointing to various passages in the music. Cellists exchanged glances without talking as they nervously tightened their bows and adjusted spikes. Beth tried to recall all that had happened since 4.30 that afternoon, feeling overwhelmed, but happily anticipating something very special. Just then, the professor approached the podium. Turning around, he tapped the baton, again, three times. Beth took a deep breath.

Immediately the room fell still. All eyes were upon him as he lifted up the Golden Manuscript, pursed his lips, then gently blew golden dust onto the transfixed orchestra. Some blinked, others coughed, each startled yet brimming with delight as it travelled over all of them. Beth giggled with wonder. The professor could hardly contain himself.

'Join me in a delectable *feast* of music!' he called brightly, ready to cast the most potent spell of all.

Lifting the baton, he raised his arms in triumphant anticipation, commanding the orchestra's full attention. At the upward flick of the baton the music commenced.

Mr Arnold played the opening passage with serious intent, followed quickly by Beth's frenzied finger work

across the keys. The professor gave rhythmic prompts, keeping her in time with the orchestra. In between, she glanced at the other players. Now the woodwind joined in as violinists plucked and bowed their strings. Very soon the hall was filled with a lively banter between the orchestra and soloists. Beautiful stringed textures ebbed and flowed well beyond the school walls. Cellists swayed as their elbows jutted in rhythmic bowing, their bodies embracing their instruments.

'*Must* be dreaming. It's a dream,' said Beth, caught up in the wonder. '*Oh*, *please* let the magic go on.'

'Where are we?' Toby spurted, losing his place.

Miss Ingle helped him keep beat by tapping her heels in time with the conductor. There were squeals of players' disbelief as Toby and Jess went on to lead, in part, the powerful dramatic tone, Toby's young ego blasting through. The conductor appeared to urge on his players, using his index finger as a second baton. As the tempo increased, pages turned with increasing speed and accuracy. During the lightest moments of the concerto, he bounced on the podium, his head bobbing sideways to exquisite harmonies. He could be heard, at times, chuckling in delight to some daft moves. His sparkling brilliance bounced off his players. Jess stared with open mouth, as notes tossed and tumbled their way across the hall. And in another magical moment the professor pulled a string of coloured handkerchiefs from his pocket, washing them over the young players and transforming their instruments into shades of blues and greens. They glanced at one another in wonder and excitement. Meanwhile, Beth and Mr Arnold cut through the mass of orchestral sound, spanning octaves and preparing for a finale that Brahms himself would have been proud of. At the final fortissimo, players' cheeks were flushed with exertion, arms ached from keeping rhythm and fingers throbbed with a pulse of musical genius. It was over.

The players slumped over their instruments gasping with wonder, while the professor cheered loudly in celebration of the brilliance of their performance. He straightened his clothing and placed the baton on the stand. A spontaneous wave of celebration consumed the players as many laughed, jumped and hugged one another. The professor threw himself into the hub of players.

'Wonderful! Marvellous!' he chanted, shaking hands before making his way over to Beth. She rose to greet him through the murmurs of excitement. Her legs were shaking.

'Thank you, *so much*, Professor! I don't know what just happened, but I want to do it all over again!'

'And *you can*, Beth,' he laughed, 'with the power of the crotchet, remember? Oh, and of course, you must *believe* you can, with your hard work and determination – without which, this would not have been possible today.'

Mr Arnold came rushing over.

'Knew you could do it, Beth! You see?'

'That was just amazing!' Beth laughed, and turned to them both as they shook hands and engaged in mutual back patting.

'Thank you, Clarence.' said the professor.

'And thank *you,* Prof.'

'It was incredible! I can't really believe it!' called Jess.

'Weren't we great!' cheered Toby, 'we were *all great!*'

'I've *never* played like that! And did you see Beth?' said Jess, standing up. 'She was amazing! *You* were brilliant Beth!' she said, waving at her.

Beth joined the friendly melee as Miss Ingle congratulated the players one by one. Some simply sat clutching their instruments, numb from their performance. Others were catching their breath and hugging each other in excitement. The violinists were busy comparing their newly coloured instruments, happy yet bewildered. Toby and Jess chatted together.

'You're not bad, you know, … I mean your playing,… I mean your music,' said Toby awkwardly.

'Really? Thanks, Tobes. Considering they told me that all I was good at was blowing raspberries!' said Jess.

'Who told you that?' said Beth, surprising them.

'My last teacher,' said Jess. But that was a long time ago now,' she said, laughing.

'Never looked back, eh?' smiled Toby.

'Beth. You were *amazing!* Join us in the orchestra!' said Jess suddenly.

'Really?'

'Yeah, Beth. Come on,' said Toby.

'You know each other?' asked Jess.

'Well, we kind of travelled here together,' said Beth quickly.

The professor was standing at the podium.

'Shhh,' said Miss Ingle, pointing to the front.

'Our music has ended for today. You were all *simply marvellous*! *Truly!* And …'

'They're *gone!'* shouted a violinist. 'The colours have gone! Look, everyone!' she said pushing her instrument at arm's length above the others.

The original wooden shades had returned, leaving no trace of the coloured hues that had transformed them during their magical performance. The others hurriedly checked theirs before turning to the professor.

'Professor?' said the violinist.

'From now on, you must *earn* your colours in *real* time.' he smiled kindly. 'Listen to the colours and look at the sound,' he smiled, 'though you *will all* remember this feeling of 'possibility' from today, you must have *your own dreams* and the *courag*e to make them come true.'

'But, how?' asked Jess. 'Surely it can't…'

'Well, for a start, what you *have* shown is your commitment to hard work to have brought you here today.'

Miss Ingle smiled, admiring his answer, and joined him at the podium.

'Remember, Rubato's his name! Let the freedom of the tempo take you to places you dare to venture to,' she said, tapping into their wonder, 'places you create in your mind, in your heart. Feel it. Believe in it. Believe in *you* and have fun!'

'Brava!' said the professor, smiling broadly. 'And you must *let* your learning happen, *not make* it happen,' he added, 'by sharing your talents freely and wholly, just as you did today. Your time, practice and intelligent work will pay dividends, leading you through *the festival of life.'*

He and Miss Ingle thanked the players as they began packing away their instruments.

Miss Ingle approached Toby and Beth. 'Please come and join our school orchestra. We would love to have you!'

'Count me in. Thanks!' Toby said, jumping in first.

'And I'd l*ove* to come,' said Beth. 'I'll talk to my mum … Oh, what's the time?' she said, frantically checking her watch.

The professor called across to her from the stage, 'Remember the pause, Beth? Mozart used to say, 'the rests mean more than the music,' he chuckled.

Beth smiled and glanced at her wristwatch.

'4.50pm *real time,'* she found herself quietly repeating.

In that moment, the professor cleared his throat, interrupting Beth's dreamy skyward gaze. He was busy writing 'homework' in her notebook next to her. Her music case stood propped against the piano stool where she was sitting, and the grandfather clock ticked through the final minutes of her lesson. He turned to her.

'See you next week. Oh, and thanks so much for your wonderful playing today!'

Beth's cheeks flushed a little. 'Don't know why he thought I did so well today.

Maybe it's the practice,' she thought to herself.

'Thanks, Professor!' she called cheerfully from the hallway, 'I look forward to it.'

Beth dropped the case into her basket, secured her helmet and straddled her bike again, humming a strangely familiar tune all the way home.

*

The following morning a young boy arrived unusually late and took a short cut through the school hall. Leaping on to the stage floor he spotted two small black objects and scooped them up.

'Curious!' he said, turning them this way and that, before popping them into his pencil case and hurrying to his maths class.

Musical Terms

8va play an octave higher

15va play two octaves higher

accelerando gradually speed up

accents emphasis on a particular note or chord

allegretto grazioso lively and gracefully

allegro a quick lively tempo

allegro ma non troppo lively tempo, but not too much

andante at a walking pace

attacca go on at once

bar music is divided into bars by vertical lines drawn on the stave, each contains a certain amount of time, divided into beats

bass clef a symbol that specifies the pitch at f below middle c

baton a thin stick used by a conductor to direct an orchestra

bell the deep inverted cup shape part of a musical instrument

bow a rod of horsehair stretched along its length, used for playing the violin, cello, etc.

bpm the number of beats per minute – indicates the tempo of a piece eg120bpm

Brahms a nineteenth century musical composer
brass section brass wind instruments
cellist player of the cello
cello a bass instrument of the violin family
clarinet a woodwind instrument with a single reed mouthpiece
clarinettist a clarinet player
composer one who creates and arranges music
concert pitch the standard pitches
concerto a work, usually in three movements, for one or more solo instruments and orchestra
conductor a person who directs the performance of an orchestra or choir
crescendo gradually gets louder
crotchet a type of note which is usually counted as the beat (quarter note)
diminuendo gradually get quieter or softer
doppio movimento double the speed
double bar line written at the end of the piece to mark the end
duet a composition for two performers
finale the last movement of an orchestral composition
fingering suggests to the player which fingering to use to play the notes

flat a symbol indicating the note must be lowered by one semitone
flautist a flute player
flute an orchestral instrument made of wood or metal
forte pedal the right sustaining pedal of a piano
fortissimo play as loudly as possible
glissando a slide from one note to another
harmonic chord a group of notes sounded together as a basis of harmony
harmony the pleasing effects of a combination of simultaneously sounded notes
key signature when a piece of music is written in any major or minor key, then the sharps or flats that appear in that key are written at the beginning of every stave, immediately after the clef
largo a very slow tempo e.g. 40-60bpm
legatissimo as smoothly as possible
legato each note flows smoothly
major scale a type of scale consisting of tones and semitones
manuscript musical notes written by hand or typed to form a musical piece
melody an arrangement of single notes in a musically expressive succession
middle C the c note in the middle of the piano board

Mozart an eighteenth century musical composer
oboe a woodwind double reed instrument
octave the interval of an eight e.g. c and the next c
orchestra a large group of instrumentalists, combining strings, woodwind, brass and percussion
passage a section of a piece of music
pause a rest
percussion the section of striking instruments e.g. pianos, drums, bells, etc
pianist a piano player
piano a large musical instrument played by pressing down keys on a keyboard and causing hammers to strike metal strings
piano pedal the left (soft/subduing) pedal of a piano
piano tuner the person who tunes pianos
piccolo a small flute sounding an octave higher than an ordinary one
pitch how high or low a note is
plop a short glissando down onto a note
plucking to pick or pull the string of a musical instrument
quaver a note that lasts half the length of a crotchet (an eighth note)
rest a symbol indicating a period of silence

rhythm the arrangement of music into beats, bars, phrases, etc

ritardando (rit) gradually get slower

rubato play with freedom of tempo

scale a series of notes arranged from low to high

score a printed/written piece of music containing the parts of all instruments

sharp the symbol indicating that a note must be raised by one semitone

sight reading reading and performing music at sight

slide the part of an instrument which slides to alter its pitch

soundboard the broad plate of wood found within a piano to reinforce the sound

spike the wood or metal point at the base of the cello, used for support and positioning

stave the five horizontal lines used for the notation of music

strings the stringed instruments of an orchestra

tempo rubato played with some freedom of time

tempo the speed at which the music is played

tie a curved line connecting two notes of the same pitch to make one longer note

time signature indicates how many beats there are in each bar and what type of note the beat is

tonality the relationship between the tones of a musical scale

tone a musical sound with reference to its pitch, quality and strength

treble clef a symbol that specifies the pitch at the g above middle c

trill a rapid alternation between two adjacent notes

trombonist a trombone player

tuning fork a two-pronged steel fork that gives a particular note when struck

turn the playing of a specific pattern of decorative notes

violin a musical instrument with four strings of treble pitch played with a bow

volante flying

woodwind wind instruments that were mostly originally made of wood e.g. flute and clarinet

Milton Keynes UK
Ingram Content Group UK Ltd.
UKHW020255010524
442003UK00007BA/76

9 781805 412496